CHEMISTRY EXPLAINED

CHEMISTRY IN USE

by
Janet Bingham

Minneapolis, Minnesota

Credits

Cover, © Vink Fan/Shutterstock; 4T, © nenetus/Adobe Stock Images; 4B, © x70tjw/Wikimedia Commons; 4–5, © NickyLloyd/iStock; 5, © Galitsyn Grigory/Adobe Stock Images; 6T, © anchalee thaweeboon/Shutterstock; 6B, © Atlantist Studio/Shutterstock; 6–7, © Bedrin/Shutterstock; 7T, © zizou7/Shutterstock; 7B, © MRC Laboratory of Molecular Biology/Wikimedia Commons; 8T, © Kedar Vision/Shutterstock; 8M, © peterschreiber.media/Shutterstock; 8B, © Sansanorth/Shutterstock; 8–9, © ldutko/Shutterstock; 9T, © MarcelClemens/Shutterstock; 9B, © MRC Laboratory of Molecular Biology/Wikimedia Commons; 10T, © Dragana Goric/Shutterstock; 10ML, © VaLiza/Shutterstock; 10MR, © Boonchuay1970/Shutterstock; 10B, © CrutchDerm2014/Wikimedia Commons; 10–11, © YinYang/iStock; 11, © ifong/Shutterstock; 12T, © chromatos/Shutterstock; 12B, © Biology Education/Shutterstock; 12–13, © New Africa/Adobe Stock Images; 13T, © Science Source/Science Photo Library; 13B, © Science History Institute/Wikimedia Commons; 14T, © LillieGraphie/Shutterstock; 14B, © ju_see/Shutterstock; 14–15, © Nick Upton/Nature Picture Library; 15, © Bearport Publishing; 16T, © Science History Images/Alamy Stock Photo; 16B, © Archive PL/Alamy Stock Photo; 16–17, © hutch photography/Shutterstock; 17, © DKN0049/Shutterstock; 18T, © Yuri Kravchenko/Shutterstock; 18B, © Fotokostic/Shutterstock; 18–19, © SOMRERK WITTHAYANANT/Shutterstock; 19B, © Public Domain/Wikimedia Commons; 20T, © petrroudny43/Shutterstock; 20B, © Dark Moon Pictures/Shutterstock; 20–21, © TinaSova20/Shutterstock; 21, © Public Domain/Wikimedia Commons; 22T, © trinset/Adobe Stock Images; 22M, © Kekyalyaynen/Adobe Stock Images; 22B, © Public Domain/Wikimedia Commons; 22–23, © dusan petkovic/Adobe Stock Images; 23, © Zamrznuti tonovi/Shutterstock; 24T, © Soho A Studio/Shutterstock; 24B, © Suzuki Leo/Shutterstock; 24–25, © santypan/Shutterstock; 25T, © Bearport Publishing; 26T, © Oleksiy Mark/Shutterstock; 26B, © MIA Studio/Shutterstock; 26–27, © SofikoS/Shutterstock; 27, © Science History Institute; 28T, © Kononov Oleh/Shutterstock; 28B, © Bacsica/Shutterstock; 28–29, © ANIS EFIZUDIN/Shutterstock; 29, © Wellcome Collection/Wikimedia Commons; 30T, © Hagley Museum and Archive/Science Photo Library; 30B, © NOPPHARAT236/Shutterstock; 30–31, © Alex from the Rock/Shutterstock; 31, © Hagley Museum and Archive/Science Photo Library; 32T, © ABCDstock/Shutterstock; 32B, © Tooykrub/Shutterstock; 32–33, © Roman023_photography/Shutterstock; 33, © Bearport Publishing; 34T, © Pavel Kubarkov/Shutterstock; 34B, © HeimatPlanet/Shutterstock; 34–35, © Ponomus/Shutterstock; 35T, © Farber/Shutterstock; 35B, © Public Domain/Wikimedia Commons; 36T, © fencifd/Shutterstock; 36B, © N_CA/Shutterstock; 36–37, © NASA; 37T, © Ajamal/Shutterstock; 37B, © University of Bristol/Wikimedia Commons; 38T, © blueringmedia/Adobe Stock Images; 38M, © gameover/Alamy Stock Photo; 38B, © Public Domain/Wikimedia Commons; 38–39, © RichLegg/iStock; 39, © Sina Ettmer/Adobe Stock Images; 40T, © Mopic/Alamy Stock Photo; 40B, © askarim/Shutterstock; 40–41, © Eric Hood/Adobe Stock Images and © Valerii Honcharuk/Adobe Stock Images; 41, © Public Domain/Wikimedia Commons; 42T, © StockPhotoPro/Adobe Stock Images; 42B, © sutadimages/Adobe Stock Images; 42–43, © KOTO/Adobe Stock Images; 43, © vchalup/Adobe Stock Images; 44, © Oleksiy Mark/Shutterstock; 45, © Mopic/Alamy Stock Photo; 47, © Bedrin/Shutterstock

Bearport Publishing Company Product Development Team

Publisher: Jen Jenson; Director of Product Development: Spencer Brinker; Editorial Director: Allison Juda; Editor: Cole Nelson; Editor: Tiana Tran; Production Editor: Naomi Reich; Art Director: Kim Jones; Designer: Kayla Eggert; Designer: Steve Scheluchin; Production Specialist: Owen Hamlin

Statement on Usage of Generative Artificial Intelligence

Bearport Publishing remains committed to publishing high-quality nonfiction books. Therefore, we restrict the use of generative AI to ensure accuracy of all text and visual components pertaining to a book's subject. See BearportPublishing.com for details.

Library of Congress Cataloging-in-Publication Data is available at www.loc.gov or upon request from the publisher.

ISBN: 979-8-89577-497-7 (hardcover)
ISBN: 979-8-89577-539-4 (paperback)
ISBN: 979-8-89577-505-9 (ebook)

© 2026 Arcturus Holdings Limited. This edition is published by arrangement with Arcturus Publishing Limited.

North American adaptations © 2026 Bearport Publishing Company. All rights reserved. No part of this publication may be reproduced in whole or in part, stored in any retrieval system, or transmitted in any form or by any means, electronic, mechanical, photocopying, recording, or otherwise, without written permission from the publisher. Bearport Publishing is a division of FlutterBee Education Group.

For more information, write to Bearport Publishing, 3500 American Blvd W, Suite 150, Bloomington, MN 55431.

Contents

Everyday Chemistry. 4

Atomic Structure 6

Molecules 8

Food Chemicals. 10

Reagents 12

Plant Chemicals. 14

Crucial Glucose 16

Soil and Agrochemicals 18

Team Nitrogen. 20

Water 22

Cleaning Chemicals. 24

Chemistry at the Pharmacy 26

Plastics 28

Clothing Chemicals 30

Construction Chemicals 32

Chemicals in Cars 34

Electrochemistry. 36

Batteries 38

Household Energy. 40

Our Lives in Chemicals 42

Review and Reflect 44

Glossary. 46

Read More 47

Learn More Online. 47

Index 48

Everyday Chemistry

From cooking an egg to turning on a light, molecules all around us are constantly changing and reacting to one another. The study of these changes and reactions is called chemistry. Chemists observe these reactions every day to learn more about the materials that make up our world. In doing so, they can put that knowledge to use in new and creative ways that help improve our lives.

A World Without Chemistry?

It is difficult to imagine our lives without chemistry. Even a piece of paper is made by changing the chemical bonds between plant molecules and hydrogen atoms. The touchscreens on many of our devices rely on chemicals that conduct electricity, such as indium tin oxide. These technologies would not be possible without the discoveries of chemists throughout history.

Scientists are still learning more about atoms every year. The large hadron collider at CERN looks for evidence of new subatomic particles.

The Birth of the Atom

People have been studying chemistry for thousands of years. Democritus was an ancient Greek philosopher who theorized that all objects are composed of small, indestructible substances. We now call those substances atoms. Democritus's ideas sparked later researchers to dig deeper into the structure of the atom.

Early Chemistry in Action

Metallurgy, the study of metals and their properties, was one of the earliest forms of chemistry. Ancient metalworkers created mixtures called alloys and found that these new substances had very different properties from the original metals. These discoveries made new technologies possible. Steel was found to be strong enough to hold up the first skyscrapers. Lightweight aluminum alloys were used to build the first aircraft engines.

Metallurgy is still studied and used today. Some modern smelters use electricity to help separate metals from ore.

Atomic Structure

All matter in the universe is made of tiny particles called atoms. Atoms contain the even smaller subatomic particles protons, neutrons, and electrons. The number of these subatomic particles determines the properties of the atom. The variety of atomic structure gives us the 118 elements we know today.

The Atomic Nucleus

The nucleus in the middle of an atom is made up of protons and neutrons. These subatomic particles are packed together into a cluster that is 2,000 times heavier than the electrons surrounding the nucleus. An element's atoms all have the same number of protons. This is its atomic number.

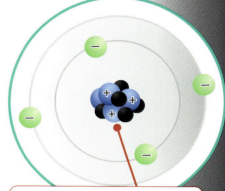

Beryllium has an atomic number of 4. Its nucleus has four protons and five neutrons. Four electrons are arranged in two surrounding energy shells.

Electrons

Outside of the nucleus, an atom is mostly empty space. Electrons—subatomic particles with a negative charge—whiz around in energy shells surrounding the nucleus. Each shell is a layer that can hold a set number of electrons, so atoms with more electrons have more shells. The equal and opposite charges of the protons and electrons in an atom attract each other, creating an electromagnetic force that holds atoms together. On the whole, atoms have the same number of electrons as protons, giving the particle no charge.

Energy shells are stacked inside one another like Russian nesting dolls. But the shells are not solid. Only electromagnetic attraction holds the electrons close to the nucleus.

DID YOU KNOW? Protons and neutrons contain even tinier particles called quarks and gluons. Scientists have discovered 36 subatomic particles so far!

Carbon 12
6 Protons
6 Neutrons
6 Electrons

Carbon 13
6 Protons
7 Neutrons
6 Electrons

Carbon 14
6 Protons
8 Neutrons
6 Electrons

Isotopes are forms of an element with different numbers of neutrons. A normal carbon atom—Carbon 12—has six neutrons in its nucleus, but other isotopes have seven or eight.

The total number of protons and neutrons in the nucleus is the atom's mass number.

The first energy shell is closest to the nucleus. It can contain up to two electrons.

As the shells fill up with electrons, more shells are added. The heaviest atoms have more than 100 electrons in 7 shells.

Bigger atoms have more shells, farther out from the nucleus. The second and third shells can contain up to eight electrons each.

Joseph John Thomson
1856–1940

English physicist J. J. Thomson discovered the electron in 1897. His experiments showed that cathode rays, or the rays seen when electricity flows through gases at low pressure, were streams of particles with much less mass than atoms themselves. We now call these particles electrons. He was awarded the Nobel Prize in Physics in 1906.

HALL OF FAME

Molecules

Atoms like to stick together! Only a few—those that make up the noble gases—keep to themselves. Most atoms bond with other atoms to make molecules. Molecules can be composed of only a couple of atoms, or they can be giant molecular structures. A crystal is a structure in which the atoms or molecules join up in a regular, repeating pattern.

Diamond is the hardest natural substance on Earth. Many of these crystals are made into jewelry, but diamonds are also used in industrial tools.

Hydrogen is a diatomic element. By pairing up and sharing their electrons to make a bond, two hydrogen atoms make a stable, homonuclear molecule.

Diatomic Molecules

There are two atoms in diatomic molecules. If the atoms are identical, the molecule is homonuclear. Elements with atoms that pair up in this way are diatomic elements. The bond is made by sharing electrons, which fill up both atoms' energy shells. A hydrogen atom has one electron, but its shell can hold two—so two hydrogen atoms share their two electrons.

Allotropes

The crystals of some elements are simple. They contain only one kind of atom. Yet they can be surprising. Their atoms join together in different ways to make different allotropes. Two allotropes of carbon are diamond and graphite. Diamond and graphite have different properties because of the ways their atoms are arranged.

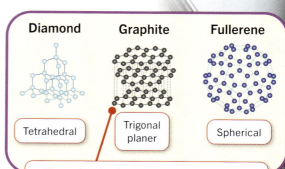

Diamond — Tetrahedral
Graphite — Trigonal planer
Fullerene — Spherical

The molecular sheets in graphite are weakly bonded, so graphite is softer than diamond, which has strong bonds in all directions. Another allotrope—fullerene—has atoms in a sphere.

DID YOU KNOW? The largest uncut diamond ever found weighed more than 1 pound (0.45 kg). It was cut into more than 100 gemstones.

A pencil drawing is made of graphite. Both graphite and diamond are giant molecular structures of carbon.

Soft graphite is used in pencils because its molecules easily slide over one another and rub off on the paper, leaving a mark behind.

Crystals of the element sulfur can be shaped as four-sided pyramids or as long needles. These different forms are allotropes.

Rosalind Franklin
1920—1958

British scientist Rosalind Franklin studied molecules using X-ray crystallography. She helped to discover the double helix structure of deoxyribonucleic acid (DNA). She also made important discoveries about the structure of viruses, as well as about the different forms of carbon in coal and graphite. Her work on carbon paved the way for the development of useful carbon fiber technologies.

HALL OF FAME

9

Food Chemicals

Like all living things, we must build and repair our bodies to stay healthy. To do that, we need complex molecules called biomolecules. Plants can create these using sunlight, but animals don't have that ability. Instead, we eat plants, or other animals that eat plants, and absorb their biochemicals into our bodies.

People with type 2 diabetes follow a careful diet to keep their blood sugar, or glucose, steady. They may take insulin to control their glucose levels.

Nutrients

An enzyme in your saliva breaks down bread starches into sugars. If you keep chewing bread, it will start to taste sweet.

A human can have 37 trillion body cells, and every minute about 300 million of them die and are replaced. The nutrients we need to do all that building are found in different food groups, so we need to combine those foods for a balanced diet. Fresh, raw foods are good for us, because many nutrients are lost during processing and cooking. But some foods, such as meat, must be cooked to kill germs, improve taste, and help us digest them.

Additives

Many foods are fortified to replace nutrients lost in preparation or to add extra nutrients. Plants do not contain Vitamin B12. It's often added to soy-based foods so vegans can still get this important vitamin. Other additives make foods last longer on the shelf or add color, taste, or texture. Additives may be natural, such as plant extracts. Others are synthetic, or human-made, such as the sugar substitute saccharin.

Curcumin from turmeric is a health food and colorant. It has carbon, hydrogen, and oxygen atoms in the formula $C_{21}H_{20}O_6$.

HALL OF FAME

Norbert Rillieux
1806–1894

Norbert Rillieux became a pioneering chemical engineer. He made sugar from cane juice by repeated evaporation at reduced pressures, producing better-quality crystals at a lower cost. This process revolutionized the sugar industry.

At least half of our diet should be fruits and vegetables. These foods give us vitamins for healthy cells, fiber to help move food through our gut, and water.

Milk, cheese, and butter give us oils and fats that our cells burn for energy. Dairy products and meats give us minerals such as iron needed for healthy cells.

For protein, we need fish, meat, eggs, or vegetable proteins such as nuts, beans, and dry seeds. These help us build and repair the cells in our bodies.

We need starchy foods such as bread, pasta, and cereals for carbohydrates. These give us energy, fiber, calcium, and vitamins. Sugary foods contain less healthy carbohydrates than starchy foods.

DID YOU KNOW? Pufferfish contain tetrodotoxin—a deadly poison. Chefs train for years and take an exam before they are allowed to cook and serve the fish.

11

Reagents

Carbohydrates, fats, vitamins, and proteins are part of our diet, and food tests show which of them are in which foods. We can use reagents, or chemicals that detect other chemicals, to do this. The tests can be as simple as adding a reagent to a food sample in a test tube and observing the color changes.

Sudden Clouds and Disappearing Blue

Lipids are fats and oils found in things like butter and cream. Scientists identify them with an emulsion test by adding ethanol to a food sample in a test tube and shaking it, then pouring it into water. If lipids are present, the liquid turns cloudy. The test for vitamin C, commonly found in fruit, uses the dark blue reagent dichlorophenolindophenol (DCPIP). A sample is added to the DCPIP drop by drop while the mixture is being shaken. If vitamin C is present, the color vanishes.

An electric water bath warms a sample to a set temperature without overheating it, but a beaker of hot water works just as well.

Changing Colors

Benedict's and biuret reagents are both bright blue solutions. Benedict's solution tests for sugars, such as glucose. It's added to a sample, and the test tube is warmed gently in a water bath. The liquid changes through a series of shades if sugar is present. The biuret test is for proteins. Two reagents—copper sulfate and sodium hydroxide—are added to the food sample. If protein is present, the blue mixture turns purple.

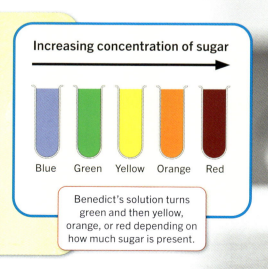

Increasing concentration of sugar

Blue   Green   Yellow   Orange   Red

Benedict's solution turns green and then yellow, orange, or red depending on how much sugar is present.

12 DID YOU KNOW? A person eating 10 carrots every day might see their palms turn orange, due to a large amount of the pigment beta-carotene.

The test for starch is a yellow-brown iodine solution. It turns blue-black in the presence of starch.

The iodine reaction happens only with starch, so we know it's not detecting sugars or other carbohydrates.

Fruits lose starch as they ripen. Some orchards use iodine tests to find the ripeness of their apples by measuring how much starch is left.

Robert Boyle
1627–1691

Irish-born Robert Boyle was the first leading scientist to carry out controlled experiments and publish the results with details about procedure, apparatus, and observation. He is most famous for Boyle's Law concerning the volume and pressure of gases, but he also introduced many standard chemical tests.

HALL OF FAME

Plant Chemicals

Plants and fungi don't seem to do much, but in fact they're busy doing amazing chemistry! There are chemical reactions going on inside them all the time. Plants have the important job of trapping energy and making glucose to build their bodies through photosynthesis. But the chemicals of photosynthesis aren't the only ones involved in a plant's everyday life.

Plant Hormones

Plants need light, and they often seek it out. They have hormones, or chemical messengers, called auxins that control the growth of their root and shoot tips. Auxins in shoot tips move away from light. They concentrate in the shadiest side of shoots and make the cells there grow faster, so the shoots bend toward the light. Auxins in root tips diffuse downward in response to gravity. This makes the cells grow more slowly on the underside of the tips, so the roots grow down.

Leaves contain red and yellow pigments, which act as sunscreen. They're hidden by the green pigment chlorophyll, so we usually see these pigments only in the fall when trees stop producing chlorophyll.

Wood Wide Web

Trees look solitary, but they share food and chemical messages as a community. Threads of fungi called hyphae link the tree roots underground, making a network called the wood wide web. The fungi get glucose from the trees and give nutrients in return, and they make a pathway for trees to share nutrients. Older trees feed sugars to seedlings, while less friendly trees send harmful chemicals. Plants are also able to know when other plants close to them are being eaten, and they respond by making protective chemicals in their own leaves.

Most of a fungus's body is hidden underground. Fungi aren't plants, so they don't photosynthesize. They break down decaying material to get to the nutrients inside.

14 **DID YOU KNOW?** The Venus flytrap can count! When an insect touches its sensory hairs, the plant counts two touches before snapping its trap shut.

HALL OF FAME

**Salimuzzaman Siddiqui
1897–1994**

Salimuzzaman Siddiqui was an Indian-born scientist who earned his PhD in organic chemistry in Germany in 1927. He studied traditional herbal therapies, isolating Indian snakeroot alkaloids, which are used as sedatives and in treating high blood pressure. Siddiqui also extracted compounds from neem tree oil to treat infections. As a chemistry professor at Karachi University, he did much to advance science in Pakistan.

Many plants contain poisonous chemicals to discourage munching. Ragwort is a British wildflower that contains toxic chemicals called alkaloids.

Cinnabar moth caterpillars feed on ragwort. The plant's toxins don't hurt them. Instead, they stay in the caterpillars' bodies, making them poisonous, too.

Ragwort can harm farm animals if they eat a lot of it, but it supplies nectar and pollen to many insects.

15

Crucial Glucose

Every living thing is constantly building up and breaking down molecules. All these chemical reactions together form a creature's metabolism. Glucose is particularly important in metabolism. It's a monosaccharide, or a simple sugar made of just one molecule.

Getting Glucose

Plants use energy from the sun to make glucose from carbon dioxide and water. They use the glucose to make bigger molecules, such as cellulose and starch. As animals, we get glucose from plants when we eat starchy foods such as bread, rice, and potatoes. During digestion, our bodies break these starches down into simple sugars, which our blood carries to our tissues. There, tiny cell structures release energy from the molecules to use in cell processes.

Very few living things can survive in the depths of the ocean around deep-sea hydrothermal vents. However, some bacteria can thrive by making glucose from the hydrogen sulfide and methane released by these undersea vents.

Green parts of plants absorb sunlight and trap its energy in glucose molecules during photosynthesis. Energy is stored in the bonds between atoms that make up glucose molecules.

HALL OF FAME

Marie Maynard Daly
1921–2003

Marie Maynard Daly was the first Black woman to earn a PhD in chemistry in the United States. Her studies focused on the role of enzymes in starch digestion and the structure and biochemical activities of the cell nucleus. Daly taught biochemistry and became a professor at the Albert Einstein College of Medicine. She also pushed to enroll more minority students in medical and scientific studies.

Making Polysaccharides

Monosaccharides join up in chains to make long natural polymers called polysaccharides. Glucose molecules ($C_6H_{12}O_6$) link up to make polysaccharides, such as starch and cellulose. As each glucose molecule links up, a water molecule (H_2O) is lost, so the polysaccharide formula is $(C_6H_{10}O_5)_n$, where *n* means any number of repeated molecules. Starch is a molecule used to store energy. Cellulose is used to build strong structures, such as those that make up tree trunks.

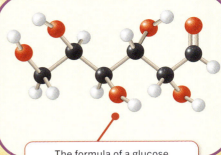

The formula of a glucose molecule is $C_6H_{12}O_6$ because it has 6 carbon atoms, 12 hydrogen atoms, and 6 oxygen atoms.

Glucose can be stored, used to release energy from food molecules, or used to make larger molecules to grow a plant's body.

Glucose is stored as starch in leaves, stems, roots, seeds, and fruit. The energy-giving, digestible nutrients we get from starchy foods are called carbohydrates.

DID YOU KNOW? The human brain accounts for around 2 percent of our weight, but it uses around 20 percent of the glucose energy needed by the body.

Soil and Agrochemicals

Soil feeds and supports plants, including those we grow for food. It is made of tiny mineral particles from eroded rocks mixed up with humus, or the rotting organic matter from living things. Both the mineral particles and humus provide important nutrients that crops need to grow. Farmers often use chemical fertilizers and other agrochemicals to help their food crops grow bigger and faster.

Fertilizers

Plants take the minerals and other nutrients they need from the soil. As each crop is harvested, the nutrients are used up and the soil becomes depleted. Farmers replace the nutrients with fertilizers, including nitrogen, phosphorus, and potassium. These release nutrients quickly, but they are easily washed away into rivers and can poison the water.

Cutting down forests or overgrazing land increases soil erosion, where the ground is worn, blown, or washed away, leaving depleted land where crops grow poorly.

Pesticides

Farmers often wage chemical wars on insects, slugs, snails, and worms that want to eat their crops. They also battle diseases, fungi, and other plants that take the nutrients their crops need. Pesticides are agrochemicals farmers use to tackle these problems. Pesticides are effective, but they can harm other nearby living things and disturb ecosystems.

Fields with only one kind of plant need many agrochemicals, because the plants have the same genes and are easily attacked by pests and disease.

18   **DID YOU KNOW?** Organic compounds have carbon-hydrogen bonds. But many people use *organic* to mean food grown without synthetic chemicals.

Some farmers plant strips of wildflowers in between crops. The flowers feed helpful insects, such as wasps whose larvae eat pests.

Organic farmers may replace soil nitrogen by adding manure and compost instead of synthetic fertilizers.

Natural fertilizers are broken down by soil bacteria, so they release nutrient nitrates slowly. Large amounts are needed to keep nutrient levels high.

HALL OF FAME

George Washington Carver
1864–1943

George Washington Carver studied botany at Iowa State Agricultural College and was the first Black American to earn a bachelor of science degree. He ran the agricultural school at Tuskegee Institute, and he realized that overused cotton fields could be restored by crop rotation with nitrogen-fixing plants such as peanuts. He also developed many other uses for peanuts!

19

Team Nitrogen

Nitrogen makes up most of Earth's atmosphere. Living things need the element to make proteins, but there's a problem. Nitrogen atoms in the air bond together strongly in pairs, and these bonds must be broken before the nitrogen atoms can form other compounds. Luckily, a team of soil bacteria helps break nitrogen atoms apart so living things can use them.

The Nitrogen Cycle

Nitrogen-fixing bacteria recycle nitrogen in the environment. These bacteria separate the N_2 atoms so they can combine in compounds called nitrates. This is called nitrogen fixing. The nitrates are absorbed by plants and used to make proteins. Nitrogen atoms pass through the food chain until they return to the soil in plant and animal waste or in decomposing bodies. Then, different bacteria recycle them into either nitrates in the soil or pure nitrogen in the air.

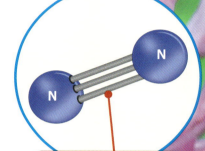

Nitrogen atoms can make three bonds, so two atoms link up with very strong triple bonds. This makes the unreactive molecule N_2.

Lightning, volcanoes, and fires also fix nitrogen by breaking apart the N_2 molecules, allowing the free nitrogen atoms to combine with other elements.

Haber Process

The Haber process is an industrial method that fixes nitrogen by turning nitrogen gas and hydrogen into ammonia (NH_3). The ammonia is made into nitrogen-based fertilizers, such as ammonium nitrate, that help farm crops grow. However, overuse of fertilizers can put too much nitrate into rivers and streams and upset the natural nitrogen cycle. Alternative methods of adding nitrates to soils are rotating crops with nitrogen-fixing plants, such as legumes, as well as the use of manure and other natural fertilizers.

DID YOU KNOW? Early Egyptian alchemists made ammonium chloride for smelling salts by heating dung and urine with salt.

Farmers enrich their fields by planting clover. Nitrogen-fixing bacteria in the clover roots turn nitrogen from the air into nitrates.

Some nitrates in the soil are converted back into N_2 in the air by denitrifying bacteria.

Decomposers and nitrifying bacteria break down the waste from living and dead animals and plants, making more nitrates available.

Nitrogen-fixing bacteria form nodules on clover roots, where nitrates build up. The clovers use the nitrates, and animals then eat the plants to gain the nitrogen.

Samuel Massie
1919–2005

Distinguished chemist Samuel Massie went to Agricultural Mechanical Normal College after being prevented from going to the University of Arkansas because he was Black. His research included developing agents to protect soldiers from poisonous gases, investigating how pollution from ships affects sea life, and studying nitrogen and sulfur compounds for treating infectious diseases.

HALL OF FAME

Water

Water may not seem very exciting, but it is a very special molecule. Whenever we run a dishwasher or washing machine, we rely on the simple chemical bond of two hydrogen atoms to one oxygen atom. This bond results in a molecule with a range of practical properties that we count on every day. The properties of the substances that interact with water are also key to water's usefulness.

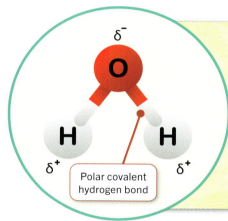

Polar covalent hydrogen bond

The Ties That Bind

Water molecules are the result of atomic bonds called polar covalent bonds. Oxygen atoms have a partially negative charge while hydrogen atoms have a partially positive charge. This difference, or polarity, of charges creates the ideal conditions for water molecules to easily share electrons through hydrogen bonding, creating a very stable molecule.

How Do We Make Water Safe to Drink?

Water treatment plants use many chemical compounds to make sure our drinking water is clean and safe. Powerful disinfectant chemicals kill bacteria and other microorganisms in water that cause sickness. Water softeners remove minerals from water that can damage pipes or make cleaning more difficult. Clumping agents neutralize the electrical charges of chemicals so they can clump together, making them easier to remove from water.

Wastewater from cities is sent to water treatment plants that use chemicals to clean the water and make it safe to use again.

HALL OF FAME

Antonie Philips van Leeuwenhoek
1632–1723

In the late 1600s, Dutch microbiologist Antonie Philips van Leeuwenhoek discovered what he called animalcules while examining a sample of pond water under a microscope. This was the first time a scientist had concrete evidence of microorganisms living in water. This eventually led to the discovery of antibiotics, or medicines that protect people from harmful microorganisms.

The heat in steam is often used while ironing. This energy breaks apart the bonds that form between fibers in clothes that can cause wrinkles.

Many household appliances use water's polarity to dissolve and remove chemicals. Because opposite charges are attracted to each other, this polarity allows water to draw other chemicals to it, breaking apart and dissolving them.

Adding heat to water increases the kinetic energy of the molecules. In a dishwasher, the energy in hot water allows it to more easily break the bonds holding food to dirty dishes.

DID YOU KNOW? Water is so important to life on Earth because it can dissolve so many chemicals, making them easier for living cells to use.

Cleaning Chemicals

A lot of washing goes on in our homes. Good hygiene means cleaning ourselves, our clothes, and the surfaces in our homes. Luckily, chemistry can help. There are some truly cool ways chemicals help keep us clean!

Plain soaps are often better at cleaning, but dyes and other additives may be used to give them interesting colors, scents, and textures.

Cleaning and Disinfecting

Water molecules tend to stick together and not to surfaces and dirt. This is called surface tension. Soaps and other detergents help clean because they are surface-acting agents, or surfactants. They reduce the surface tension of water so it can stick to dirt on other surfaces. Some household cleaning products also contain disinfectants to kill germs and sterilize surfaces. Bleach, a whitening agent that removes stains and kills germs, is a solution of chemicals including sodium hypochlorite (NaOCl).

How Soap Works

A soap molecule has two halves with different properties. It has a soluble, hydrophilic head that's attracted to water, and a hydrophobic tail that repels water but attaches to the fats and oils in dirt. The hydrophilic end dissolves in the water in the washing solution, while the hydrophobic part sticks to dirt. As we scrub soapy water into our skin and hair, the soap molecules lift the dirt and break it up into small structures called micelles that are then suspended in the water, ready to be rinsed away.

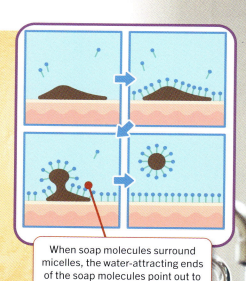

When soap molecules surround micelles, the water-attracting ends of the soap molecules point out to the water, and the water-repelling ends point in to the dirt.

HALL OF FAME

Lloyd Augustus Hall
1894–1971

Lloyd Augustus Hall was a Black American inventor who held 59 U.S. patents on methods of preserving food, including one for a way to cure meats by combining table salt with other sodium salts. He realized that some spices introduced germs and made food go bad. He found a way to sterilize the spices with ethylene gas in a vacuum chamber. This idea was later used by the food, drug, and cosmetics industries.

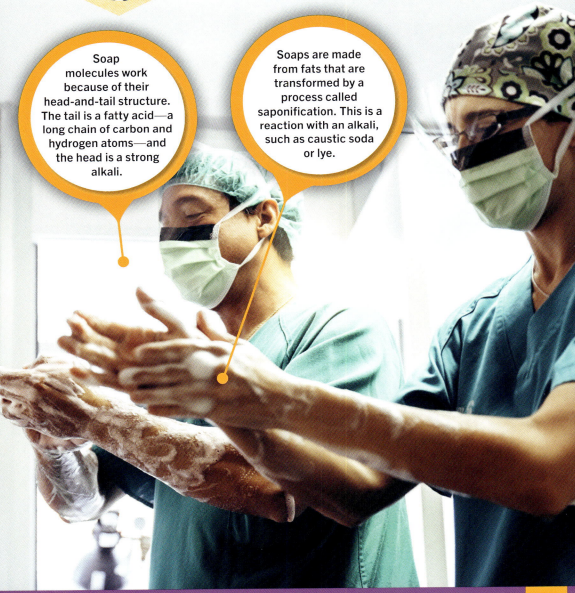

Soap molecules work because of their head-and-tail structure. The tail is a fatty acid—a long chain of carbon and hydrogen atoms—and the head is a strong alkali.

Soaps are made from fats that are transformed by a process called saponification. This is a reaction with an alkali, such as caustic soda or lye.

DID YOU KNOW? People have been making soap for at least 5,000 years. Potash was made by steeping wood ash in water, which then reacts with fat to make soap.

Chemistry at the Pharmacy

Medicines help us get better when we're sick. But the wrong medicine, or the wrong amount of one, can also make us ill. Pharmacists are trained to be both chemists and health care professionals. They prepare the drugs that doctors prescribe and give advice about over-the-counter drugs.

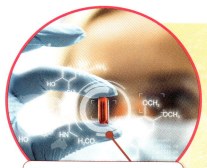

Most medicines are now made by pharmaceutical companies, which means they can be produced in large quantities in clean, safe laboratories.

Development of Medicines

Ancient people discovered herbal remedies when they noticed that eating certain plants made them feel better. Many of our drugs originally come from natural sources. Aspirin is based on salicylic acid from willow bark, while penicillin was discovered in a mold called penicillium. Modern drugs are carefully tested to make sure they are effective, safe, and prescribed in the right quantities.

Vaccines

Most people get vaccinated against diseases such as measles, mumps, and rubella as children, and they get more vaccines as they grow older. Vaccines protect the body against infectious diseases by mimicking the virus or bacteria so the immune system is ready to fight when it meets the real infection. Normally, it takes 5 to 15 years to develop a vaccine. During the COVID-19 pandemic, international scientists worked together and mapped the chemical sequence in the new virus's DNA in just 10 days!

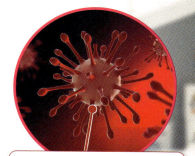

The COVID-19 virus is one of many coronaviruses. Scientists' knowledge of the makeup of other viruses helped them to develop a COVID-19 vaccine in just one year.

DID YOU KNOW? A snake's venom can contain more than 100 compounds. Scientists use some of them to treat pain, cancer, and disorders of the heart and kidneys.

Antibiotics kill bacteria that cause infections. Doctors prescribe them only when necessary, because some germs are developing resistances to antibiotics. Using fewer of these drugs can help stop this process.

Over-the-counter drugs often treat minor problems, such as coughs, colds, allergies, and skin disorders. Pharmacies also sell medicines that doctors prescribe for more serious health issues.

Pills can be made to be swallowed, chewed, or dissolved in water. Capsules have a coating that dissolves in the stomach to release the medicine.

Companies give their medicines different brand names, but each medicine is also known by its chemical name.

HALL OF FAME

Percy Lavon Julian
1899–1975
Percy Lavon Julian was a Black American chemist and director of chemicals development at the Glidden Company. His research included producing versions of plant compounds called steroids in the laboratory for use in medicines. He made physostigmine for treating eye disease, and he developed large-scale production of cortisone drugs and the hormones progesterone and testosterone.

27

Plastics

Plastics are polymers. Their molecules are long chains of smaller molecules called monomers that polymerize, or link up in a repeated pattern like beads on a necklace. Polymer molecules have a backbone of linked carbon atoms with atoms of other elements branching off them. Some common polymers include polystyrene, polyethylene, and PVC.

Versatile but Problematic

Plastics are tough, light, waterproof, and flexible. They can be formed into films, sheets, or foams that can be made into all sorts of objects from bottles to medical equipment. They are everywhere, and that can be a problem. Waste plastics hang around for decades or even centuries, sometimes breaking down in the oceans into pieces smaller than 0.2 inches (5 mm) long. These harmful microplastics are swallowed by sea creatures, introducing toxins into the food chain.

Products made of natural polymers such as corn starch are biodegradable and can be recycled into fertilizers.

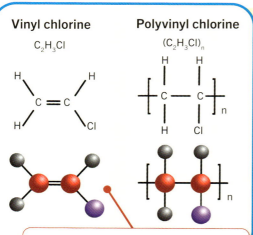

A vinyl chloride molecule has just six carbon, hydrogen, and chlorine atoms. Its chemical formula is C_2H_3Cl. The formula of the polymer PVC is $(C_2H_3Cl)_n$ where *n* can be any number of C_2H_3Cl molecules in the chain.

Polymerization

The monomer vinyl chloride (VC) is a gas that polymerizes to make the strong plastic polyvinyl chloride (PVC), which is used to make pipes. The secret of how a monomer like VC polymerizes lies in the double bond between its carbon atoms. This double bond can break to make single bonds. This means the two carbon atoms remain joined by a single bond, but each of them can also link up with a carbon atom in another VC molecule. This happens many times, joining any number of VC molecules into a chain.

HALL OF FAME

Alexander Parkes
1813–1890

The first manufactured plastic was invented as an alternative to ivory and tortoiseshell when demand began driving elephants and turtles toward extinction. British chemist Alexander Parkes made cellulose nitrate by dissolving cotton fiber in acid and mixing it with vegetable oil. He patented this as Parkesine in 1862. It was later developed into celluloid, which made everyday items like hair combs cheaper and available to more people.

Even recyclable plastics can be recycled only once or twice before they degrade too much to be useful. In the end, they cause pollution just like single-use plastics.

Scientists are working to develop alternatives to plastics, as well as ways to break down existing waste plastics into reusable chemicals.

The Global Ecobrick Alliance turns waste plastics into ecobricks—bottles stuffed with other waste plastics that can be used in construction.

Everybody can help fight the plastics crisis by following the reduce, reuse, recycle rule. But recycling alone can't solve the problem. We all need to become less dependent on plastics.

DID YOU KNOW? Every minute, around one million plastic bottles are sold around the world. More than 40 percent of all plastics, including these bottles, are thrown away after one use.

Clothing Chemicals

Clothes are important. They keep us warm, but we also wear them for fun and to show our personalities. Most clothes are made from textiles, or fabrics made from fibers and threads that might be woven, knitted, or felted. Turning them into clothing involves several chemical processes, many of which have an effect on the environment.

Synthetic Materials

Human-made fibers, such as nylon, polyesters, and acrylates, are polymers made from chemicals extracted from fossil fuels. Like other plastics, they are not sustainable, and they don't decompose, so they cause pollution. Scientists are looking for better, more environmentally friendly ways to produce and recycle polymers.

It is fairly easy to make nylon with limited resources. All it takes is mixing its monomers in a flask. Long nylon polymers form, creating a threadlike strand.

Natural Fibers

Wool, cotton, and silk are natural polymers. Cotton is made of plant cellulose, while wool and silk are animal proteins. They are renewable, sustainable, and biodegradable. But even natural fibers must be processed to be used. Wool fibers contain fats and dirt that are removed with detergents and other chemicals before dyeing, which also uses chemicals. All of these chemicals can cause pollution if they are not disposed of carefully.

Silk threads come from the cocoons of silk moth caterpillars. Cellulose from plants like lotus and bamboo can be made into a vegan alternative.

DID YOU KNOW? It can take up to 2,200 gallons (8,300 L) of water to make just one pair of cotton jeans!

Many synthetic fabrics are cheap to produce and cheap to buy, so they are often quickly thrown away.

Elastane, also known as spandex, is a stretchy synthetic fiber used in sports clothes. The latest elastane fabrics adjust the fit and strength of their grip as the wearer moves.

The fashion industry has a huge environmental footprint. It produces 10 percent of global carbon dioxide emissions—a greenhouse gas that contributes to climate change.

Engineers at the Massachusetts Institute of Technology have developed a polyethylene fiber that draws sweat away from the body. The technology could be used to recycle plastic bags into sports fabrics.

HALL OF FAME

Stephanie Louise Kwolek
1923–2014

Stephanie Louise Kwolek was an American chemist who researched synthetic polymers and fibers for the DuPont company. She developed a flame-resistant polyamide fiber, sold as Nornex. She also invented industrial fibers including Kevlar, a material five times stronger than steel, which is used in bulletproof vests and spacecraft.

31

Construction Chemicals

Materials such as cement, bricks, asphalt, metals, wood, coatings, glass, and gypsum are used to construct everything from bridges to roads and skyscrapers. Construction chemicals include adhesives, sealants, coatings, insulation materials, composites, and concrete admixtures.

Road-building asphalt is a mixture of aggregates and a liquid binding agent called bitumen, a sticky substance produced from crude oil.

Concrete and Cement

We see gray, stonelike concrete in buildings everywhere. This material is made from a mixture of aggregate—crushed rocks—and cement. Cement is made from minerals such as limestone and contains calcium, silicon, aluminum, and iron. It's mixed with water to make a paste, which coats the concrete aggregate and acts as a binding agent. Newly mixed concrete can be formed into shapes, and it hardens to be strong and lasting. Admixtures are other ingredients added to improve concrete, such as styrene butadiene rubber.

Composites

Composites combine two or more materials into a substance that's more useful than the starting materials alone. For example, steel reinforcing, or rebars, gives concrete extra strength and flexibility. Nanocomposites contain nanomaterials—tiny materials measured in nanometers. The nanomaterial graphene is a single layer of graphite just one carbon atom thick. Newly developed nanocomposite coatings made of lime with graphene can help keep temperatures stable inside buildings, saving energy.

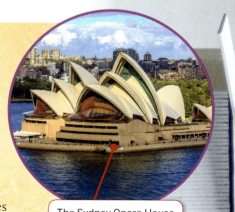

The Sydney Opera House is built from steel-reinforced concrete.

DID YOU KNOW? The Three Gorges Dam in China is made of 37 million cubic yards (28 million cubic m) of concrete, which took 17 years to pour!

Chemicals in Cars

Most cars use gasoline or diesel fuels made from crude oil. These fossil fuels are finite—they will eventually run out and we can't replace them. In addition, burning them produces climate-changing carbon dioxide and pollutants. Scientists are developing clean, sustainable alternatives, such as biofuels, hydrogen fuels, and electric vehicles.

Diesel fuel is made from less volatile, longer-chain hydrocarbons than gasoline. It's cheaper to produce and more efficient, but it creates more carbon dioxide, sulfur, and other pollutants.

Gasoline

Gasoline is made from the short chains of hydrocarbon molecules found in crude oil. Short-chain hydrocarbons are volitile, meaning they have a low boiling point. That makes them ideal for making energy in vehicles. These molecules of hydrogen and carbon are mixed with molecules that have longer chains and must be separated out to be used. The shorter molecules are separated out by boiling the crude oil at different temperatures.

Biofuels and Electric Vehicles

Biofuels are renewable fuels produced from organic waste and crops. Biofuels emit fewer polluting emissions, but crops grown for fuels may destroy land. Electric vehicles do not burn fuels to run. But they run on batteries that are often charged with electricity originally made from fossil fuels. Also, batteries are made from precious metals that are currently difficult to recycle.

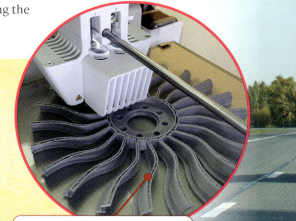

Computer software can 3D-print car parts by depositing layers of melted plastics or metals. One day, this could make cars lighter and less environmentally damaging.

DID YOU KNOW? One single electric car battery requires the same amount of materials as can be found in 300 smartphone batteries.

The combustion reaction of gasoline with oxygen produces carbon dioxide and water plus energy. But incomplete combustion in cars also produces carbon soot as well as carbon monoxide gas.

Pistons inside a car engine's cylinders move down to take fuel vapor and air into the combustion chamber. Then, the intake valve closes, and the piston moves up to compress the gas.

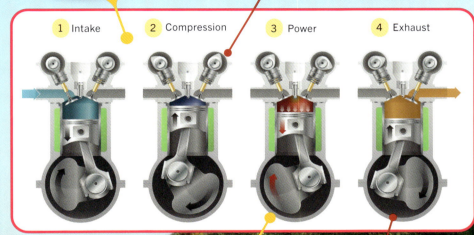

1. Intake 2. Compression 3. Power 4. Exhaust

A car engine's piston movements cause spark plugs to fire under pressure, igniting the fuel. Fuel can ignite too soon, so antiknock additives like MMT are often added to fuel to help it ignite at the right pressure.

The turning crankshaft converts heat into mechanical energy. The combusted gases and pollutants leave the car through the exhaust pipe, and the cycle begins again.

Gertrud Johanna Woker
1878–1968

The Swiss biochemist and pacifist Gertrud Johanna Woker studied and taught at Bern University. She warned of the dangers of leaded gasoline and condemned poison gas, germ warfare, and atomic weapons. Books she wrote were burned by the Nazis. She experienced much sexism in her career and was denied the title of professor for more than 20 years, but she is now recognized as one of the most influential women in chemistry.

HALL OF FAME

Electrochemistry

Electricity is an important part of chemistry. It's the result of a charge carried by electrons or ions—atoms that have lost or gained electrons. When charged particles flow, we get electricity, and when they flow around a circuit, we get an electric current. Some chemical reactions produce electricity, and others use electricity. This is electrochemistry.

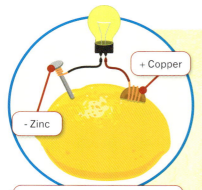

A lemon can be turned into a weak battery because the citric acid in the fruit acts as an electrolyte, capable of carrying a charge between electrodes and completing an electric circuit.

Electrolysis

Electrolysis is splitting a compound by using electricity. It needs an electrolyte, or a liquid containing ions, as well as a positive and a negative electrode. The electrolyte may be a melted solid or a compound dissolved in water. When a current passes through it, the positive and negative ions are pulled in different directions toward the electrodes, and the compound gets torn apart. Electrolysis of sodium chloride dissolved in water breaks the molecules into hydrogen, chlorine, and sodium hydroxide, which are used in many industries.

Galvanizing

Iron and steel corrode as they react with oxygen in the air to form iron oxide, or rust, which weakens the metal. To protect these metals, objects made of iron or steel are galvanized, meaning they are coated with protective zinc. Galvanizing items by dipping them into molten zinc produces a thick, long-lasting, protective coating. Galvanizing with electrolysis, called electrogalvanizing, is less expensive and produces a thinner coating, which is smoother and shinier but not as hard-wearing.

These steel grids are electrogalvanized with zinc to protect against rusting.

DID YOU KNOW? Experiments in the field of electrochemistry inspired the writer Mary Shelley to create her famous character, Frankenstein's monster.

Batteries

Many modern electronic devices, appliances, and cars rely on electrical energy. But not every electric device can be plugged in at all times. These devices need a way to store energy for later use. They rely on batteries that convert chemical energy into electrical energy.

Converting Chemicals to Energy

Each battery is filled with two chemicals that react to each other and release electrons when the battery is plugged into a circuit, a device or series of wires that create a path for electrons. As electrons move through a metal wire, they carry their negative charge with them. This causes a positive charge, or current, to move in the opposite direction from the battery's positive end to the negative end.

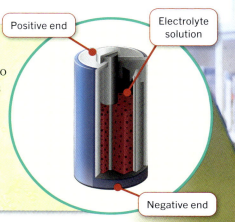

Positive end

Electrolyte solution

Negative end

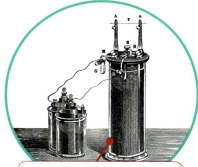

Gaston Planté invented the first rechargeable lead-acid battery.

The Life of a Charge

The first usable batteries were created in the 1800s. These batteries worked only until the chemicals inside had finished reacting to each other, and they worked only once. The first rechargeable battery was introduced in 1859. Early rechargeable batteries could be used multiple times but held less charge over time. Newer rechargeable batteries last much longer.

HALL OF FAME

Akira Yoshino
Born 1948

Akira Yoshino is a Japanese chemist who shared the 2019 Nobel Prize in Chemistry with two other chemists. He designed the world's first commercially viable lithium-ion battery in the early 1980s. Lithium-ion batteries are more durable and charge much faster than traditional lead-acid batteries. This helped make small devices, such as mobile phones, much more affordable.

Sodium-sulfide batteries have been used to store energy from wind and solar farms so the energy can be used when the conditions are not right to generate this energy.

New electric devices have batteries that require less frequent charging than earlier versions of the same devices.

Many elements in batteries, such as lithium, are not renewable. There is a limited amount of them on Earth. Chemists are looking for alternatives that can be easily made and reused.

DID YOU KNOW? A battery-powered electrostatic bell at Oxford University, known as the Clarendon Dry Pile, has been in use since the 1840s.

Household Energy

Most of our household energy comes from fossil fuels. But scientists are creating new ways to generate energy. These include geothermal energy, which is drawn from heat within Earth, and nuclear energy, which splits uranium or plutonium atoms to release the energy stored within their nuclei.

Researchers in Cambridge, UK, have designed ultra-thin artificial leaves that turn sunlight and water into clean fuel as efficiently as plants. These flexible devices could one day create floating solar farms.

The Sun's Energy

Plants trap the sun's energy through photosynthesis. We can use that stored chemical energy by burning fossil fuels or biomass, such as wood or kitchen waste. We can also harness the sun's energy through solar cells. Since sunlight won't ever run out while the sun exists, solar energy is a sustainable source of energy.

A hydroelectric facility pumps water uphill into a reservoir. When released, the stored water flows downhill, turning a turbine to generate electricity.

Nonrenewable and Renewable Resources

Nonrenewable energy is energy taken from resources we can't replace. There will be no new fossil fuels once existing crude oil, natural gas, and coal are gone. Renewable energy comes from resources that don't run out or that can be replaced. Energy stores that can be used without being used up are called sustainable energy sources. Power plants currently use a mixture of nonrenewable and renewable sources to generate electricity. As society moves toward cleaner, more sustainable energy, everyone can help by saving energy wherever possible.

DID YOU KNOW? Some experts say more than 90 percent of the world's energy could come from renewable resources by 2050.

HALL OF FAME

Hennig Brand
Around 1630–1710

Hennig Brand was a German chemist who longed to find the fabled philosopher's stone, an object that alchemists thought could turn cheap metals into gold. He believed human urine was the key and collected all his friends' urine to help his search. He didn't find what he wanted, but he did become the first person to discover an element. He found a white material in urine that glowed in the dark and called it phosphorus.

Turbines and paddles in the ocean can turn the constant motion of the ocean waves and tides into electricity. The energy is renewable, clean, and reliable, but the equipment used can harm existing ecosystems.

Solar panels contain photovoltaic cells that generate renewable electricity from sunlight. One day, new technology may allow us to turn entire rooftops into giant solar cells.

People often burn wood, crops, and organic waste materials to generate electricity. These biofuels and biomasses are sustainable, but farming biofuels can destroy ecosystems or farmland.

Wind turbines turn their blades to face the wind, capturing kinetic energy from the wind, which is converted into electricity and fed into the power grid.

Our Lives in Chemicals

We use chemistry every day, even if we don't know it. At mealtimes, enzymes in our stomachs break down the complex molecules in our food, much of which was grown using chemical fertilizers. And when we turn on our devices, chemical processes send electricity through metals to allow them to work. Chemists are improving these technologies every day.

Where Do Chemists Work Today?

There are many kinds of chemists. Some study chemicals and perform experiments to discover their properties in order to create new ways to harness chemicals. Production chemists take these new discoveries and apply them in practical ways. They often help create new medicines or build the parts that go into the latest electronic devices.

Better Batteries for Clean Energy

Solar and wind energy are growing industries around the world. However, the weather isn't always sunny or windy enough to make the energy needed by many power grids. Luckily, chemists are working on new kinds of batteries, such as flow batteries, that can store extra energy to use on those days. Flow batteries pump two chemical liquids past each other, allowing ions to flow between the chemicals. This generates an electrical current that can be used when needed.

Green Chemistry

Green chemistry is a growing branch of chemistry that investigates new ways to safely create and dispose of chemical products. Some chemists are studying new ways to use agricultural waste and plant oils as raw materials for renewable energy. Others are developing microbes that will speed up how quickly commonly used plastics degrade.

43

Review and Reflect

Now that you've read about the uses of chemistry, let's review what you've learned. Use the following questions to reflect on your newfound knowledge and integrate it with what you already knew.

Check for Understanding

1. How is an atom structured? Where are the protons, neutrons, and electrons located? *(p. 6)*

2. How are diamond and graphite similar? Why do they have different properties? *(pp. 8-9)*

3. Why are nutrients important to the human body? *(p. 10)*

4. What is a reagent? What are some ways we use them? *(pp. 12-13)*

5. How do auxins encourage growth in the shoot tips of plants? What about in their root tips? *(p. 14)*

6. What are the benefits to pesticides? What are the drawbacks? *(p. 18)*

7. Describe the nitrogen cycle. *(p. 20)*

8. List some of the ways people use the chemical properties of water. *(pp. 22-23)*

9. How does soap work? *(pp. 24-25)*

10. What are antibiotics? What is antibiotic resistance? *(p. 27)*

11. Explain how a vinyl chloride (VC) molecule can become a polyvinyl chloride (PVC) molecule. What is this process called? *(p. 28)*

12. What are composites, and how are they useful to construction? *(p. 32)*

13. What is the process of splitting a compound by using electricity called? How does it work? *(p. 36)*

14. In what ways are modern batteries different from the first batteries ever created? *(pp. 38-39)*

15. Name three types of renewable energy sources. *(pp. 40-41)*

44

Making Connections

1. Consider the ways animals create biomolecules in their bodies and how plants create them. In what ways are animals and plants dependent on one another to create these molecules?

2. What is polarity? What is the importance of polarity in a water molecule?

3. What is the difference between synthetic and natural materials? List one of each found in this book and compare their properties.

4. List two different ways cars are fueled. What are the benefits and disadvantages to each? How are they similar to each other?

5. What are three different ways electricity is used in chemistry? List them and describe how each process works.

In Your Own Words

1. Which of the common uses of chemistry in this book interested you the most? Explain how it works. How could you learn more about this concept?

2. Compare and contrast the discoveries of two different people featured in the Hall of Fame sidebars. How have their discoveries contributed to the science of chemistry?

3. There are quite a few inventions that exist only because of chemistry. Choose an invention in this book and imagine what would have happened if no one had discovered the chemical process that made the invention possible. How would the world be different?

4. Many chemists are inspired by nature when creating new advancements in science. Pick a feature of a plant or animal you know and explain how you could transform it into a new technology.

5. There are many chemical functions in this book that are helpful to people but harmful to the planet. List some of these harmful chemical functions. Then, compare them with alternatives that do the same job but cause less harm. What are some ways you can use these less harmful chemical functions in your day-to-day life?

Glossary

acid a chemical with a value lower than 7 on the pH scale

alkali a chemical with a value higher than 7 on the pH scale

atom the smallest unit of a chemical element

atomic number the number of protons in an atom

carbohydrates a group of organic chemicals including sugars and starches

chlorophyll a green pigment in plants that absorbs light and turns it into chemical energy via photosynthesis

compound a chemical made from the atoms of more than one element

crystal a solid material with its particles joined together in a repeating pattern

dissolve when a solid is mixed with a liquid

distillation a process in which a mixture made up of liquids with different boiling points can be separated

DNA deoxyribonucleic acid, a long molecule found in cells that carries instructions for the structure and function of living things

electron a negatively charged particle found in an atom

element a chemical made of a single type of atom

formula the way scientists show the number and type of atoms present in a molecule

fossil fuels energy sources, such as coal, crude oil, and natural gas, that are made from the remains of plants and animals that died long ago

ion an atom that carries an electric charge because it has lost or gained an electron

isotopes forms of an element that have different numbers of neutrons

mineral a naturally occurring inorganic solid with a defined chemical structure

molecule a group of two or more atoms that are chemically bonded

monomer a small molecule that links up with others like it to form a larger molecule called a polymer

neutron a particle with no charge found in the nucleus of an atom

nucleus the center of an atom

photosynthesis a process that uses water, carbon dioxide, and energy from sunlight to produce food for plants in the form of glucose

polymer a chain-like molecule made of repeated smaller molecules

proton a positively charged particle found in the nucleus of an atom

Read More

Dingle, Adrian. *My Book of the Elements (My Book).* New York: DK Publishing, 2024.

Jackson, Tom. *Matter & Energy (The World of Physics).* Minneapolis: Bearport Publishing Company, 2025.

Ting, Jasmine. *Green Energy (A True Book: A Green Future).* New York: Children's Press, 2024.

Van Vleet, Carmella. *Electricity: Circuits, Static, and Electromagnets (Build It Yourself).* Norwich, VT: Nomad Press, 2022.

Learn More Online

1. Go to **FactSurfer.com** or scan the QR code below.
2. Enter **"Chemistry Use"** into the search box.
3. Click on the cover of this book to see a list of websites.

Index

acids 13

agrochemicals 18

alkalis 13

atomic numbers 6

batteries 34, 36–39, 42

biochemistry 16

cars 34–35, 38

cleaning chemicals 24

clothing 30

combustion 35

construction chemicals 32

COVID-19 26

crops 18–20, 34, 41

crystals 8, 10

diamonds 8–9

DNA 9, 26

electricity 4–5, 7, 34, 36–37, 40–42

electrochemistry 36

energy 6–8, 11, 14, 16–17, 23, 32–35, 38–43

energy shells 6, 8

evaporation 10

fertilizers 18–20, 28, 42

food 10–12, 14, 17–18, 20, 23, 25, 28, 34, 42

fossil fuels 30, 34, 40

gasoline 34–35

glucose 10, 12, 14, 16–17

graphite 8–9, 32

insulation 32–33

matter 6, 18

medicines 22, 26–27, 42

metals 5, 32, 34, 36–38, 41–42

monomers 28, 30

organic 15, 18, 33–34, 41

pharmacy 26

photosynthesis 14, 16, 40

plants 4, 10, 14–23, 26–27, 30, 33, 40, 43

plastics 28–30, 34, 43

pollution 21, 29–30, 33

polymers 17, 28, 30–31

reactions 4, 14, 16, 36

reagents 12

recycling 29, 34

soaps 24

soil 18–21

space 6, 37

sunlight 10, 16, 39–41

vaccines 26